MY FALL FROM GRACE

My Fall FROM *Grace*

The Gospel of a Sinner
Amber Dawnel Doyle

PALMETTO
PUBLISHING
Charleston, SC
www.PalmettoPublishing.com

My Fall From Grace
Copyright © 2024 by Amber Dawnel Doyle

All rights reserved

No portion of this book may be reproduced, stored in a retrieval system, or transmitted in any form by any means–electronic, mechanical, photocopy, recording, or other–except for brief quotations in printed reviews, without prior permission of the author.

First Edition

Paperback ISBN: 979-8-8229-4635-4

Contents

Dedication vii

Introduction 1

Chapter 2: My Children 4

Chapter 3: A Message, or Just a Dream? 10

Chapter 4: Friendship, Learning, and Relapsing 14

Chapter 5: The Hidden Cross 19

Chapter 6: What Strength Does a Person Have? 23

Chapter 7: The Standoff of Love
between a Father and Daughter 29

Chapter 8: A Needed Rest and More Learned Lessons 40

Chapter 9: Thor's Hammer and Forgiveness 52

Chapter 10: My Person 56

Chapter 1:1: My Beginning and My Twin Flame 60

Humanity Challenge! 69

Dedication

There have been many people in my life who have helped shape the person I once was and the person that I am becoming now. No one person is less or more significant than the other. That is why I have decided to dedicate this book to many. My family, who have always been a guiding light. Even in times of darkness, they have always forgiven me and continued to teach me to be a better person to myself and to others. I grew up knowing who our Lord was because of them.

My children, whom I love and cherish with all my heart, have shown me what tough love is, but it has made me realize that even as parents, we can become the students of our own children, especially when we forget the values that we once taught them.

To my friends who have become family, even the ones in death, turning the water into wine ourselves, who show proof in our own veins, with love that we all share for each other. Those friends may or may not be present now, but that wine never leaves, and neither does love.

To all of humanity, I am so grateful to see all the beauty within you all. The differences and cultures that make us different but the same, as our Lord's children. We are all in his image, all backgrounds and races, all religions that know of the Creator of all things (no matter what name you learned to use).

And to one very important man, Mike Diechman. He was my mentor, and unfortunately, he passed away this year. There are few people who we can say are extraordinary people, but he was one of them. Mike Diechman had faith in who I was and taught me to see that in myself. Even after I left his company, he never stopped guiding me, and he taught me what it meant to be a leader, to lead by example, and to take ownership when your team fails. He taught me to take ownership over my own life and my failings, showing me how to overcome those failings just by making an effort to change them. I was in rehab when he passed away and during his funeral. I know that he knew what I was battling, and I know that even though I disappointed him and many others, they are proud of me now of who I am becoming. When Mike died, the whole community cried. I only hope to be just as extraordinary as he was by helping others in the many ways he did.

I also dedicate this book to all those whom I have known and the ones whom I have never met, who have lost their lives to addiction. I have lost many friends this past year, and I finally understand the pain that tormented them for so long. I know they all sit at our Lord's feet, completely cleansed and at peace in his light.

MY FALL FROM GRACE

Even though I can't dedicate this book to just one person, above all I dedicate it to our Lord because he has been the greatest teacher of them all.

Don't let me forget my old man, the Great Gatsby, who died this past year too.

The beauty that our animals bring to our lives is extraordinary. They love us unconditionally, and without even speaking the same language, they know our love, and we know theirs. That is beauty and a gift from God. Our Lord has also given me the beautiful knowledge to know that it was him that placed every person and thing in my life at the right moments, whether to teach me or to just be there, because he knew that is exactly what I needed at those very moments.

Thank you to all those that are reading this book now and to all those whom I have mentioned. You are all part of me and I of you. *We are all a family of one with many different colors of the most beautiful rainbow.* The gold at the end of that rainbow isn't gold at all, but instead it's something that shines one hundred times brighter. That, my friends, is unconditional love for each other, no matter what pasts or differences we share. Find that end to the rainbow, and you have found the heaven that God created for us.

Introduction

We typically begin a book with an introduction that explains what you are going to read in a briefing of words. Your chapters follow, one after another, until the end is reached. My chapter 1 explains exactly where my journey began and where it is leading me, but it's not where you would typically find chapter 1. With that said, I am simply going to explain why it doesn't begin after the introduction, and then I will end the introduction with a simple question, and you will understand exactly why I chose to write my book in this way, whether it is now or later.

Everyone should understand what the Alpha and the Omega truly are. It is the beginning and the ending of all things. The Alpha and the Omega is the Lord himself, the Creator of all things, the One who began all things and can end all things, and he is the One who can write and speak all things into existence. Remember, though, that our Creator has the power to write or speak it into existence, but he can also unwrite it and replace the words he spoke, as it is his choice and his alone. With that said, you cannot have a beginning without an ending, yet you cannot have an ending without a beginning, no matter what he chooses to write or unwrite. Just as the humorous question we all ask ourselves, "What came first, the chicken or the egg?" The answer to that question is the Creator. He came first and created all things through his vision and words, and he spoke them into existence. In other words, it doesn't matter what came first, but instead it matters to know he created them, and they exist through him.

My beginning doesn't start after the introduction, but instead it comes at the designated end of my book. You can begin reading chapter 2 after the introduction or flip to the back of the book and read chapter 1, only to come back and read chapter 2 until you finish at the designated end. It is your choice. Just as our Lord gives us the divine right to choose, I ask you this very question: "Will you skip past the end to read the beginning, only to come back and read chapter 2 until the designated end, or will you start with chapter 2 after this introduction and read all the way through until you finish with my beginning?" I love new beginnings, so even at the ending, I can begin once again. It is your choice and your choice alone. I recommend that the beginning will only come at the ending because even in death, it's a new beginning for us all. What will you choose? Beginnings can be extraordinary, challenging, and sometimes scary, but they can be powerful and life-changing in extraordinary ways, nonetheless. I challenge you to be fearless. Wait until the end to start

MY FALL FROM GRACE

a new beginning. Let's begin, no matter what your choice is, because it is your choice either way.

Chapter 2
My Children

𝒯his is not only a chapter but a letter as well. My boys, you should know how exhausted I am and that I have been fighting as hard and as long as I could. I am so sorry that I disappointed you. If you are reading this, then you should know that I am no longer here as I once was, but not in any way because I stopped fighting. My mind and body just simply gave out, and I was carried by our Lord the rest of the way. He is still carrying me now. He has been restoring me and my body into something greater than I ever was before. Even though I am different, I am still the mother that you remember. He is still healing me as you read these words. I want you boys to know how much I love you and how truly blessed I am to have such wonderful boys. That love for all three of you is what made my heart beat again and my lungs fill back up with air the night that I died.

MY FALL FROM GRACE

It was not five minutes after I was brought to the place where I was saved in Christ that death came upon my body. I felt my soul leave my body as it went limp, without a heartbeat, and no air was coming in or out of my lungs. It felt as if I were being electrocuted from my legs all the way up until it reached my heart, stopping it instantly. It was your little brother's voice that kept my soul next to my body. I heard and watched him as he went from door to door asking for help, each door closing in his face. I felt his pain as he shook my head back and forth, screaming, "No, Momma, no!" I believe God sent me to that very spot that I delivered food to just the week before. I never noticed the pole that was in the center of the street. It wasn't until that night that I was guided back to that very spot. It is where I finally noticed it had a sign taped to it. That sign about Jesus is what made me hang my head and beg to be saved.

What was more extraordinary was what led us there. The lights on the roads and highways began to get brighter as we got closer to each one, so I followed them to that very sign. That road is off Highway 33, which leads into Greenville. I remember how bright the lights were because they hurt my eyes as I'd approach them. You turn right as you are coming into Greenville or left as you are leaving. At the end of that short road is where you will find that pole with that message taped around it. At the end where the pole stood, you could look left and see the apartment with the number 217. That is where I delivered food to just the week before. To the right, that is where I pulled into and drove to the end and stopped so I could turn around to go home.

The very spot at the end is where I took my last breath that night. Your little brother will always be a witness to this testimony. As painful as it was, it was also a miracle to remember.

My soul was not attached to my physical body any longer, and I began to beg, "Please, not now, not yet! He needs me! I can't leave him like this! Please!" A few moments later, Alan was back inside the truck, and I could still hear his screams and his pain. It was in this moment that something beyond this world hit me so hard right in the chest, and it brought breath back into my lungs. It was a hard breath, as if I had just swum up from the deepest depths of the ocean and took a breath for the first time. I cried because I knew I had been given another chance. I had been given another chance to be your mother and a chance to right the wrongs that I created all around me. It was almost as if the people who shut the door in your brother's face knew what was about to happen. Like they already knew I was drowning, yet I would somehow find the strength to swim to the top, like a child learning how to swim for the first time.

With this new breath and new life, I had been given a new responsibility; I just didn't know what that was yet. Even though my body was still filled with the drugs that tainted my mind, I felt clean from my head to my toes. Baptized in the Holy Spirit and fountain of youth, were the waters that I swam up from. After that, I followed where he led me, and even if I wasn't ready to put down the drugs, I knew our Lord was present.

MY FALL FROM GRACE

I believe your brother will one day, and even you two boys will be spiritual leaders. I saw how strong your brother was that night; even at my own fault, the Lord showed him his miraculous will to take away or give new life as he decides. Afterward, we began again following where the lights led us, until we stopped at some apartments. I am still not sure why those apartments were important, but we parked in the front because we only had three miles left on the gas tank. I did not know how we would get home, but I knew we were OK and being watched over by our Lord. Then a message came to my mind that said, "Be wise, old owl," and I knew exactly what to do. I spoke the words to Alan, and then I pumped my brakes three times, at which seventy-five miles of gas appeared on my gas tank. That was more than enough to get back to our camper safely. Alan saw this small miracle and yelled as he rejoiced. He said, as he shook my arm, "Momma, it's a miracle," and we both began to cry again. It was a miracle, and we both witnessed it for the second time. It was the first time I had ever seen your brother rejoice for our Lord, which was my fault that I had not taught him sooner of his glory. God showed us both that evening.

Afterward, we drove home, and Alan and I went to bed. What happened next is for another chapter, but I say this to all three of you: You are born with hearts that love as deeply as my own. Don't ever let anything, not even me, take away that love that shines through you. I am grateful for your tough love and knowledge in knowing right from wrong. Even as my own children, you have taught me as the mother that sometimes, tough love is necessary. Remember this, though: Even when someone that you love hurts you, disappoints you, or angers you, it's OK to have those feelings. Take the time you need to heal from wounds that your loved one caused. Show them the same tough love that you feel is necessary, but just don't forget that once you are strong enough from the pain inflicted, you may need to go help pick them up off the ground. The pain and fear of loneliness can be far worse and more painful than any drug. Everyone can fall, no matter how high they have placed themselves, but what is hidden behind the lies and disappointments is what really brought them to their knees. Sometimes, it's worth asking, "Why? What really brought you to your knees?" Behind the drugs and lies is the truth of the pain. This is where you may understand that what you see on the outside is only the picture. What's within is what has destroyed that person initially. Find out what it is within them that hurts them even more. That's where they need the most help. Those are the demons that they've been left to fight alone. Never give up on your loved ones, because there is always a chance.

Take time away when you need to heal yourselves but be strong enough to go back and make sure that they are OK. I am sorry I didn't teach you that, but I am grateful for your teachings as the child to the mother, nonetheless. You are strong kids, and I know you are each meant for greatness, in the best possible ways. I am so proud of you. You all have a light in you that comes from within to love everyone unconditionally. That is the light of our Lord. One day you may forget, and I pray and know that even if it's your own children who remind

MY FALL FROM GRACE

you of what is right and wrong, you will learn, just like I have. From the top to the bottom and from the bottom back up to the top. That's what we do!

Chapter 3

A Message, or Just a Dream?

The night that my youngest son and I returned after such miracles that the Almighty had given to us, we were both exhausted, mentally and spiritually. We both went right to bed, and it didn't take long for us to fall asleep. That night, I had a dream or message, whichever you choose to believe, from the Almighty himself. It was one of confusion, but the words were spoken very clearly. I awoke not understanding why, or how, I would do what he had asked me to do. I knew deep down that I was still an addict and not living the way he would want me to live. I was still seeing darkness and pain all around me.

In his message he stated, "You are to go before my people in Israel and tell them that it is time." He did not explain what that meant, and I did not ask. It was as if I knew that those words alone would be understood by those he asked me to say them to. He went on to tell me, "The Rapture has already begun, and you will not be going when the others do. You are to stay behind and lead the others into glory." That told me that even the ones who don't go when he calls them home will be given a second chance. He also told me, "Your sons will become spiritual leaders that help guide the rest of them until you all come home." That was all he said, and I awoke, frightened yet concerned that I may not be worthy of such a task.

I thought to myself, "Why would he choose me, the sinner that has hurt myself and others?" To be sure, there is someone more glorified to do such a task. I also began to think, "How would I even get to Israel to see his chosen people and speak those words to them?" That same morning, with much dread on my mind, I opened my emails to find a letter from a senator. The first part of the letter read, "I understand your concerns about Israel, and I am working with them very closely." How could this be? Was it just a coincidence or a scam? I looked it up online to see if similar letters or scams relating to the same topics existed. Whether they existed as a scam or not, it was quite a coincidence. My mind did not rest, and my anxiety grew stronger over the next few days. All I could see around me were evil things that just didn't make sense, things that scared me to my core.

It was just a few days later that I went into town to check my mail at the post office box at Staples in Greenville. As I was leaving, my heart began to feel stressed and in a like way that it did the night I was saved twice by our Lord. I came to a stop at an intersection in Greenville, and my son had to call the ambulance. I knew I needed help, and I didn't want to die. That day at the hospital, I was imagining the worst things someone could imagine, and that was the night my son was placed in the custody of the state. My son went to the care of my mother, and I went to rehab for the first time.

It was at Holly Hill that I discovered just how lost my mind was, but it's also where I began getting better and meeting incredible people. Those people at Holly Hill all had different reasons for being there, but they all had something special to offer me. This is where I met a girl who had the ability to speak to those that we've lost. She was incredible, and I knew when she shared with me certain things, that my Nanny or grandmother was there with me. My Nanny was a classy woman, and she always would say, "Hey, shug." I remembered her voice for the first time in many years. That girl was a special girl, and I felt exactly who she was. I also met a rocket scientist who had his own struggles, but he became a friend, and I had no idea that we both would learn so much from each other in the few weeks to come.

I met a beautiful soul who had seen so much pain in such a small amount of time, and she looked to me for guidance. I simply told her to find her warrior within, giving her a new name in life. That name was "Ruby Warrior," and I think about her often. All the other people there were wonderful humans, just suffering in different ways than my own. I still pray for all of them and their healing. The staff…boy, do they get it hard from the patients, me included. They are amazing at what they do. Without them, who would be there to help guide us back in the right direction in life?

MY FALL FROM GRACE

This chapter began with my dream and brought me to my first rehabilitation center. The reason I bring you to this place in this chapter is because of the rocket scientist and former marine. We became friends, living only miles apart. It's also where the demons began to disappear. Our friendship is what leads to my next chapter. I had no idea I would lose such a good friend only two months later.

Chapter 4

Friendship, Learning, and Relapsing

After Holly Hill, I began my friendship with the man who was a retired marine and a rocket scientist. I went the following day after my release to his house to pick up his truck and then to go back to Holly Hill to pick him up. I had no idea how much of an impact he would have on my life at that time. We became friends very quickly, and he showed me a lot of history in Cherry Point that I didn't quite understand at first, but I knew it meant something to me. I am not sure why they named that place, Cherry Point, but if you look up the spiritual meaning "cherry" in Christianity, you will understand why I felt such a connection.

This is also the time that I learned of my mentor's passing. My friend helped me through these initial days. He told me about his mentor, too, and they both shared the same name but were from different places. There is something in that name: Mike. He was a great teacher and an extraordinary man. I was also digging deep into my own family history as well as his. It gave me something to do and to keep my mind busy. Sean was doing the same thing. I believe our families must have met in a past life at some point. The girl at Holly Hill who spoke of my Nanny even said that we were kindred spirits. Some may believe that means that we were meant to be together, but I believe it means that we were just meant to cross paths, however briefly.

During this time, I learned that my family helped shape this very state and possibly even states around us. I have a long military lineage that dates back to the Revolutionary War and possibly even before they came to this country. It was amazing to see how many of the men were named Thomas. I found the very first census, with names included that ranked in prosperity from top to bottom. Now my family's name was just a few down from the top, but what brought tears to eyes was how the census was determined. You see, each family name included the number of people in the family, and the very last line included the number of slaves that each family owned. That's part of the way they determined your wealth. My family name was near the top, but unlike the others listed, the last line showed *no* listed slaves, and it presented zero. With tears of joy as I am typing now, I realized my family didn't believe in slaves, so they owned none! This was amazing to know because the people that worked with them were free men and women. They worked as a family unit. My father told me this years ago but it never actually sunk in until I saw that census. How glorious that is to say! I am so proud of all my family descendants for never choosing to own what was never theirs. We are all God's children and are not to be owned by anyone or anything. They loved the people they worked with so much so, that when slavery ended, they adopted our family name. There are many black Strouds to this day because of the righteousness and love that my family had in their hearts. I would love to meet some of them because they will forever be a part of my family.

My friend was also learning about his history and how our families may have crossed paths years before. One night, God spoke through me in a language that many would say was speaking in tongues. You see, speaking in tongues is speaking God's language, but you must have an interpreter. My friend was the interpreter. The one universal language that God has shared with everyone on this earth is mathematics and the beauty of numbers. Numbers mean everything. From frequencies, to energy, to building and creating new medicines, you will find mathematics and numbers. Each position is given the gift to comprehend what numbers, frequencies, and formulas are needed to complete or create a task given by God. Even though I didn't understand the numbers and patterns I was seeing and speaking, the rocket scientist and my friend did. He knew—and I believe with all my heart—that for the very first time, he saw God's grace through me. Can you imagine someone of science and numbers understanding that God created us all? He did, and even though our friendship wouldn't stay long, because my journey through Christ was just beginning, I still prayed for him and his healing every day.

After that night my relapse began, and at that time, I did not know that I would never see my friend again. It was so overwhelming to see God's hidden truths, and at the same time, I had to face my demons that I had masked with a drug that made me not feel the pain. I was afraid and still in pain, so the drug helped, but at the same time, it began to destroy my relationships all around me. I went back to my mother, and the demons began to arise once again. It was as if I had a choice: I could run, hide, or face them head on. Like I was fighting the armies of demons that the angels themselves said would fight for us. I chose to fight. I fought hard, and my mind went to places that were dark yet freeing.

I was angry at God for condemning Satan himself. I felt as if the dark angel, who is also God's creation, was imprisoned for far too long. At the same time, I was battling the losses in my life that continued to tear me apart. I wanted to give up and give in to the darkness so it could finally take my breath for good. I was weak and lay there many days in confusion. A thought came to me as a vision, and it was a simple question: "If you had the choice to save twenty-one thousand souls or all of them, what would you choose?" I didn't even hesitate, and I answered, "I would save them all." I began to cry every day because I didn't know how I could save them all. Me, the sinner who was sick with darkness—how could I do such a task?

The following days were hard, and I began to fight with my loved ones who were providing shelter for me, my son, and my cats. I began to wonder and walk to different places. In one instance, I drove to Greenville, but I never made it because my truck began to stall, so I pulled down a small road, off Highway 17, and parked. At the end of that road, is where I really saw God and the demons within myself. I felt as if I were being led by God himself to see things that only I could see. This brings to my next chapter.

Chapter 5
The Hidden Cross

At the end of the road, which was hidden in between the beautiful trees that surrounded it, I came to a stop at a gate. It was like a gate that would bear a sign that would typically read, "Keep Out" or "Hunting Land." It did not bear a sign, though. It was free to walk into, so I did. As soon as you walked in and to the left, there was a small creek. It was hidden in the trees, but behind it there stood a large cross. All around the very small creek were beer cans and other trash that others had left behind. It was a solemn place for someone, or many, to go to. Maybe to let go of what was hurting them, or maybe just to talk to God. I saw it as a message that even the addict can find God and be healed.

I continued my walk until I came to a fork in the path. I decided to go right, and just a little way down, I looked left into the woods. There was clearing in the center, so I decided to go in. I saw the patterns in all the trees. They reminded me of the chalice, Christ's cup, that we all drink from. The blood of Christ is what fills that chalice that we all drink from, and I began to cry. I pictured my own brothers hanging from the same cross that our Lord died upon, and I yelled and screamed at God. I was angry that the innocent were hanged because of sinners like me. Even though it was his choice, I wanted to take my brother down and place myself there. I imagined that if I could just do that now, it would circle back in time to heal the innocent with my own wounds.

I embraced a tree and begged God, the only one who has the power to turn back time, to take me instead. I begged him to use my blood to heal his wounds. I wanted to fight the demons all around me, so I began to. I fought until I had no energy left. I knew I was failing. I did not have that power. So I left that clearing, leaving my phone and my keys. I thought they'd be there when I returned. I walked on a little farther and found another clearing. In the center of that clearing was a tall bush, almost a tree, and I looked at it as if it were Satan himself. I thought that with the might and will of God, I could burn it down myself. Once again, I failed. I lay down in that clearing, exhausted by the heat, and thought to myself, "God is going to destroy us all with the heat of the sun for not taking ownership of all our own sins." I lay there in the heat and somehow tried to bring all the heat from the sun into my own body. I thought if I could learn to withstand the heat and bring it into my body as if it were a solar cell, I could save the rest of us, even if it killed me.

MY FALL FROM GRACE

My body was so hot, but it began to cool as if I were a greenhouse. It was healing my wounds. I finally stood up, and out of nowhere, something hit me on the head. Not literally, but it still hurt, and I could see what was thrown from the heavens directly at me. I picked up a book that wasn't there, and I flipped it over. The title of that book was *The Never-Ending Story*. I broke out into laughter, and yes, I said to God, "You jerk." I could imagine in my mind God asking, "What did you think you were doing by trying to kill such demons?" I looked at him, as I then remembered an old movie that I had watched, with the star of the show being Jim Carrey, and then said aloud, "What does it look like I am doing? I'm kicking my own ass."

Now before you get upset with me because of the way I speak to our Lord, just know that I do apologize, and I have gotten better with my tongue. He is all things, and the way I look at it is: if we are his reflection, then he is our reflection too. That means that he is also the comedian who can be an ass at times when he is trying to teach a good lesson, even when they are hard lessons to learn. I beat the hell out of myself in those hours. So my comedian, the Almighty, was teaching me that I can't fight an army of demons alone, especially when they are the demons that I trapped within myself. I wasn't built to do that.

So I stood before that bush that I imagined would burst into flames and I said, "Forgiveness." One by one, I began to forgive each demon that I held within myself. If I can't beat them, I can forgive and set them free. So I let go of each one, each pain that I held within myself. Each one that left was extremely painful, and I had to forgive even myself for trapping them there. The last one was the hardest to let go of. It was the serpent himself that had wound himself around my spine and made a home from the only place I had given him to hide. Now, I won't speak of what that serpent did to that little twelve-year-old girl, but I ripped that serpent from my body, leaving myself limp as if it were the spine holding up my posture itself.

I somehow found the strength to lift myself back up and held that serpent in front of me. I looked him dead in his eyes and I said, "I forgive you, and I forgive the one who did the same to you." I cried with love for the serpent because I knew that he was holding onto that twelve-year-old girl inside myself, not to hurt her but to protect her from the generational curse that haunted him. I love my serpent now, and with that forgiveness, I set him free. I watched as he went home, back into the woods that held the cross of his brother too.

Letting go of demons and forgiving them can be just as painful as trapping them in the hells that we create within ourselves. I felt a loss because they had been there for so long. My eyes bear the mark of the serpent so that I will never forget his true beauty that was given to him by our Lord. We are his creations, and we are not to condemn, not even the serpent himself. My journey was not over that day, and the walk that began after is what begins my next chapter.

Chapter 6

What Strength Does a Person Have?

As I began to leave those woods, exhausted and thirsty from the heat, I started looking for my keys and my phone that I had left behind. I knew exactly where I had placed them, but they were no longer there. It was if God wasn't done teaching me that day. As hot as it was, I began walking toward my truck, which was still parked at the gate. I had no idea how I was going to call for help to get a ride home, but I had a sense of peace and strength that I did not have when I entered those woods.

I walked along the highway toward some homes that I saw in the distance. It was so hot, almost like the world would burst into flames because the sun came too close to the earth that day. I stopped for a rest next to a light pole, and I imagined shooting an arrow up into the sky, just to let in a little rain, so it would cool the earth. Silly me… could I really have that kind of strength? It didn't rain at all that day. Go ahead and laugh. I did! I did have one passerby who stopped and asked where I was going and if I needed a ride. I told him I was going to Havelock, and he politely said, "I'm not going that direction." He then left me there, so I began to walk further down the road toward a house on the left. It didn't look as if anyone was home, but I gave it a chance anyway. I went up to the house and knocked, and I was right: no one was there.

So my walking continued. I was still at peace, just taking in all the beautiful things around me that were God's creations. I noticed that there would be a cross or something favoring God in each home I passed. That gave me even more peace to know that at least I was surrounded by homes that provided safe havens for those that loved Christ. Of course, no one was at those homes during that part of the day. They were likely at work, as it was during business hours. The farther I walked, the more the homes in the distance looked miles away. There was a path to the left that I came to that led through half an open field, and the other side was wooded. I could see that on the other side of that field, there was a house in the distance. A choice was given to me at that moment. I could either continue walking straight or take the path to the left and go to the house that seemed the closest. I chose the path and began another walk, as I absorbed in all the beautiful countryside.

The path started out straight and then took another left as it rounded some trees and then went straight again, bringing me up

MY FALL FROM GRACE

behind the back side of the home. It was beautiful, and it reminded me of an old-style farmhouse, but it was brand new. As I approached, I was met by a very cute but fierce dog. He was protecting his home, and I was a stranger who came out of nowhere. I stood very still as he approached. He barked and showed me his teeth as if he were the lion himself, protecting his pride land. I took my time, never turning my back on him, and step by step, I walked forward, and with each step, he lunged. I talked to him as if he were an old friend and he had just forgotten who I was. He didn't care, ha-ha. His hair stood straight up, the closer I got. I was afraid, yet I wasn't.

I approached the stairway to walk up so that I could ring the bell. I noticed a few work vehicles there, so I thought maybe someone was home. When I got to the top step, I noticed an exceptionally large nail just lying there, as if it were placed there strategically. I picked it up and thought only of Christ and the nails that hung him to the cross. My peace was still there, but I began to mourn for him again. My brother in the flesh, and the nails that helped crucify him until death. I put the nail in my pocket and walked to the door. I noticed all sorts of shoes lying at the front door, so I imagined a good family living there. Of course, no one was home, and I had a very protective dog at the bottom of the stairway. What was I to do? I slowly walked down each step, and he stopped me at each one. So then I decided, if he isn't going to let me leave this exact spot, I'll just sit and wait for someone to come home. I sat for about ten minutes, just looking around and taking everything in. There was another dog that seemed more friendly, but it was chained up and could only reach the back side of one of the work vans.

Eventually, the protective lion of a dog walked over to his friend and began to play. Was this my moment? I could try to run, but I had been bitten before, so I decided to slowly approach the friendly dog. That dog was magnificent in size and was white with long fur. We greeted each other, and at that point, the protective lion of a dog became calmer. Not a friend yet, but not so aggressive. As I stood there, I noticed an opening in the trees to the left. One of the trees had some red writing on the outside. I could not make out what the words said, but I thought it interesting nonetheless.

With a heart that loves to wander and the curiosity of a cat, I entered the open wood line. Its path was circular, as it rounded back out to the other side, and as I went in, I noticed broken dog collars lying along the path. The first thought that popped into my mind was a scene from my favorite series. That series had a dragon queen who broke the chains and collars of the slaves that she saved from their masters. I remember the collars being thrown to the ground and then some being thrown at the slave owners. Why that popped into my mind, I wasn't quite sure at that point. As I kept walking, I found more nails, broken tools that help build homes, trash that looked as if it were left over from building a house, and some other things. I am not sure why, but as I walked, I picked up this trash and things left behind. It was as if someone were leaving those things there for me to find.

I walked out of one side of the woods, still holding all these things, and then entered the other side, where there was another opening. On that side, I felt dread and a sense of death almost. I didn't want to be on that side. I did notice what looked as if it were a tiny animal cage without a top but circular in shape. The tiny door to the cage was open, and to the left is where I gently laid all those things, as if to lay them to rest on a mound of dirt. I left that side of the woods quickly, and as I did, I noticed that the homeowners were finally home. I approached, but I didn't see the dogs. I tried to explain why I was there and what I was doing, but I could not find the right words to tell them. They looked at me very strangely and snickered a little at the crazy lady who had wandered onto their property. I apologized and asked if I could use their phone, which they allowed me to do.

I called my mother, and she said she would come get me. The young man who owned the home then offered to take me back to my truck, but I declined and said I would keep walking. The peace of being outside surrounded by all the beautiful things that God created seemed to keep me grounded that day. Before I left their home, he asked me if I knew the gentleman who had also appeared on their land just a few days or a week prior. He said he couldn't remember his name, but he thought it was Joshua or something like that. I said no and smiled. To this day, I don't know who the man was he was referring to, but I hope to understand one day who he is and what took him to that place as well.

As I walked down the street, a sheriff stopped to see if I was OK, and I said yes. Of course, he had to run my background, and when all was clear, he gave me a ride to the nearest store to wait for my ride. I didn't have to wait long, and after being picked up, I went back to my truck and waited for a tow. The tow came and took my truck back to my mother's, and we rode home. I was still at peace but still very confused about the day. That night would begin my first time with God that would be much different from the days before, or any time in my life, really. As we go into the next chapter, please remember that my questions to the Lord himself were never questioning his words in scripture or those of Christ himself. I take you into the next chapter, as a child who was upset with her father and had the strength to question him, yet a heart that would understand the lessons that were being taught.

Chapter 7

The Standoff of Love between a Father and Daughter

After my venture into the woods, twice in one day, and at two different locations, I had quite a mixture of emotions. In my mind, I was angry at myself and us, as a society, for allowing ourselves to drink the blood of the innocent. I felt it was being used as a crutch instead of as a remembrance. I was angry at God for not forgiving his other son, the fallen angel, and one of his children either way. I was angry at myself and us as a society, for continuously blaming the devil for all our sins that we commit, all the way back to Eve. I was angry at myself and at society for judging others on many different levels.

I thought about Christ himself being hung from a cross for our sins, and even though he did that for us, why did we allow it to continue, even to this day? Yes, he gave his life to save us all, but did we have to continuously hang him back on the cross just to be saved once again? We imagined it, read about it, and even spoke it back into existence, repeatedly. Why do we have to condemn all those who believe differently than we do, or condemn the ones who call the Almighty by a different name? Does it make them wrong? Just because their cultures taught them his name and teachings a little differently than our own. I questioned whether the King James Version of the Bible was the stonework of the word. I was angry at myself and even society for thinking that we, on either side of any teachings of the Almighty, are the ones who are right and the other wrong.

Was I not allowed to question our Lord and ask these hard questions? Was I not allowed to do my own research and even learn bits and pieces of the language of the first original words of God? Who gave the men at the council of Nicaea, in AD 325, the right to decide what books and teachings of Christ would or would not be included in the Bible? Weren't they the leaders of that time? Am I supposed to just accept what they said was the word? I thought you could not add or take away from the word of God. Did they not do that very thing when choosing what was more important and what was to be left out? Did they have their own agendas? Why can't we, as a society from around the world, do our own research? It's there to find, right?

MY FALL FROM GRACE

Would I trust a bunch of congressmen, with their own agendas in mind, to give me a book in which they have declared the Holy Book itself? Go ahead, laugh a little; it's OK. I wouldn't trust a bunch of politicians to decide either. Those men in AD 325 were no different, yet they were just as human and still the children of the Almighty, just like us today. They were sinners too. I even questioned God on how we can condemn those who love their partners, even if they are the same sex.

I know by now that many of you are sitting there reading this very chapter, and in your minds, you are already coming up with a way to justify any of these questions that were tearing me apart inside. So before you get upset, let me explain why I questioned God himself and looked directly to him for the answers. You see, that's where we got it all wrong. Yes, there is a book that is a guide to the divine, which, right or wrong in interpretations, is a guide. So let me ask you this question: Do you truly have a relationship with the Almighty and ask for guidance directly from the source, or have you just memorized passages and verses in a book? Do you yell and scream and stomp your feet and then ask for forgiveness afterward, if you think your life should be going in one direction, yet what you asked for wasn't given? Think of it like this: we are all children of God. Whatever name you use, the Almighty is the Creator of all of us. If you are a parent, or even a family member of a child, can you not think of a time when your child was angry or upset because they didn't understand why things were the way you were teaching them, no ifs, ands, or buts about it? How are we any different? If Lucifer himself, the most beautiful angel, was also a child of God, and when he was cast out of heaven for wanting to sit in his Father's chair, did it change the fact that he was his Father's son? No, it did not. And how foolish of us all to think that God, even in his anger (please remember, at this point, your anger as a parent, teacher, or guide when those you meant to teach or rule didn't listen) wouldn't forgive his fallen son? Would you cast out your son or daughter for all eternity, if they simply meant to wear your shoes and looked up to you so much that they wanted to be just like you?

Let's take it back to Eve. Did Satan himself deserve to be condemned alone for tempting Eve with the apple? Where is the ownership? And when did we decide that all our sins, even today, are Satan's fault? Where is the ownership from Adam, who decided to eat with his wife, when he, too, could have said no? Did that make Eve become the serpent herself at that point? Didn't God, the Almighty Creator, Allah, Yahweh, the All Father, Anu, Mother Earth, or whatever name you use, gift us with the divine right to choose? The answer is yes! We were gifted with the divine right to choose whether to love our Creator or not, to listen to the word of God or not, or to commit the very sins that we are tempted with every day, or *not*!

I remember when my children were young and one would get into trouble; they'd blame the other within seconds of getting caught. Did you punish just one child, or did you recognize that both were just as guilty, even though only one child was talked into doing the crime? My kids are laughing at this point and know exactly which one talked the other into doing what he knew he'd get in trouble for. We as the children ourselves have been doing this for far too long. I asked God that question, as to why he forgot about his son below our feet, and he answered me. What I learned by asking was that we have been blaming Satan for our own mistakes for far too long. We trapped him in hell, inside all of us, by using him as the scapegoat and then drinking the blood of the innocent to escape our own torment. We are not vampires, though, and we still choose to eat the apple and commit our own sins, whether tempted or not.

It's easy to blame others, but any good leader will teach you about ownership and taking responsibility when your team fails. God still loves Lucifer, and I believe he has forgiven his son already. We keep him trapped here, within ourselves. That's what the broken collars in the woods were all about. We made ourselves slaves by not taking ownership. Any fallen child who has been either thrown out of the house or left because they didn't want to follow the rules forgets all anger or what made them angry to begin with. Especially when that door opens back up and the tears from the Almighty or parent begin to fall, cooling us from the inside out.

Let's reverse this: Have we as parents not learned from our own children at times, when we forgot the very core values we taught them? Did we admit to our children that we were wrong, or were we too prideful because we were the parents and what we say goes? Did Christ himself not remind the Almighty of the love he had for all his children, right or wrong? Forgiveness, remember? We learn from the top of the house all the way to the bottom and back to the top if need be. Would you spend time with your brother if you were just as guilty? I would, even if that meant spending some time in the fires of hell so that our brother could finally come home too. Don't our military members even declare this? Never leave anyone behind-no matter what, they must walk into, to save the lives of their brothers and sisters serving alongside them? I may not have been a part of any military branch, but I am from a long line of military members and warriors from the past, so it runs in my veins.

I declare this: my sins were many, but they were my own, and I would stay behind if I had to, even if it meant saving the first son and beautiful angel of God himself. When heaven comes down upon us, I will stay behind until every soul knows the love that the Almighty has waiting for each one of us. Would you do the same? Wouldn't you reach down into the bottom parts of your soul and decide you would stay, too, and teach it again and again if we have to! That's what we are supposed to do right? No man, woman, or any being left behind? I'd sit next to the dealer who sold me the drugs, if it meant reducing some of his time. Think about it. Would there even be a drug dealer if there wasn't an addict? So I am just as guilty? Absolutely!

Would you do some of the time for the brother or sister you taught to shoot and put the gun in their hand, if a crime was committed because of it? Some may say we do time on the outside when our loved ones are locked away. That is a true statement, but deep down, those who did the crime with them or because they in some ways were associated, think, "I'm glad it wasn't me who got caught." You may or may not suffer in silence, but what "time" are you really doing with them? Could we not change this and do some time with our brothers and sisters, some who are locked away far longer than others, because they had court appointed attorneys or no money? What if we could, as a society, do some of the time with them, never admitting what we are doing "time" for or what part we played? Because let's be honest: the only real judge in life is the Creator. What if a law were passed, and it simply stated that you could choose to go into the very jails they sit in and do some of that "time" for them? Without having to explain why, but take off some of their sentences, because it should be rightfully shared. Would anyone in the world—from the top, where our leaders sit, to the bottom, where you have the addicts and dealers, and bartenders who served the drink to the man who killed someone on the way home that night? What about the very judges and lawyers who sit and either help defend, convict, or judge the ones behind bars? Are some of them just as guilty for driving while drinking, some with drug habits or other addictions that they kept secretly hidden? Would they come down from the top levels of the legal pyramid and do some time with the very men and women they convict?

What about the officers who commit crimes themselves, but because of their own brotherhood, they have each other's backs? Would they go sit next to the alcoholic they locked away, knowing just the weekend before that they, too, were driving drunk? I must believe within my heart that if all of us were given the choice to reduce the time of a fallen brother or sister, without having to admit what we were guilty of, we would absolutely do this! This works on all levels of life.

God was not angry at me for questioning him, because if I had not, I wouldn't have discovered that hell doesn't exist but is within our own minds and hearts. I wouldn't have looked back in time and seen my own brother's face sitting up on that cross. Or my other brother burning in the fires of hell. After all, Lucifer is a child of God too. I wouldn't have taken off my own shoes and walked through the thorns and on the hot pavement for days, until I could not take it anymore, if I had not asked that very question. I wouldn't have looked up at our Creator and said, "Please don't let the innocent bleed for us any longer, and let the blood on my own feet heal the wounds of his."

I thought about the ones who were so looked down upon because they loved a partner of the same sex, and then I thought, "I am a worse sinner than they are." How could I not believe in our Father enough to know that he has the power to tip the scales back if too many loved the same sex and couldn't bear children to continue with his family? What about the children that are left without parents, and need someone to care for them? Adoption is just as beautiful. Isn't he powerful enough to undo what he wrote or spoke into existence himself? How could I not understand that before? Aren't we all his reflection? Both man and woman? We are *all* the reflection of our Lord. Man or woman, lion or tiger, beast or serpent, tree or flower, angel or fallen? *All* are the reflections of the Creator who looks down upon us, so doesn't a reflection show both yourself and the Almighty? How can you say to just love only one part of yourself? We must look up and see that the Almighty is us *all*, as well. The many-faced God himself, within our own reflections? He doesn't just love the ones that love him. He loves all of us, regardless.

You cannot love only one side of yourself, because a heart needs all sides to beat. *We all* are the reflection of God, and he is *us all*. So if we cannot love one another for whatever differences that we see in each other, both good and bad, then we do not love God fully. We must love each other and all things because it is the Almighty that we see in the reflection. All of us as one. We are all his temple and his church, and he could not exist safely within, if any part of the house or church were forgotten, left behind, torn down, or fallen.

What does the Trinity or the triangle look like when it shines down into its own reflection? It looks like a square and just like a church that needs all four sides to make it a strong church. We are that reflection and without seeing that the triangle needs to become the square holding both sides of the triangle perfectly within it. This is what needs to happen to make it the church that the Bridegroom himself needs to come home to. He is ready to see his bride. This is what he was showing me.

The weeks in which I was learning these lessons were hard, and even more so, my body was exhausted. When spiritually awakening from any darkness to the glory within us all, we can find it exhausting but worth it, once it begins. I began to realize we are all slaves here, but of our own doing. It's us that keeps us here, and remember that sometimes we have to face the demons and forgive them, and then we can see the light that even they can hold. I saw the mark of the beast. There are many marks, and we have them stamped on our very own foreheads and don't even notice. I had many marks that were revealed. I will not cast judgment on any other person and tell you what might be on yours. That is something you will have to look for within yourselves to see. My marks came in the form of the dollar sign, the word *addict*, the word *pride*, and even the word *love*. My demons were my own, and even they taught me some hard lessons that led me back into the light.

If you think about the dollar sign, what makes a dollar sign? If we take it back to the Garden of Eden and think about the perfect one who took the first bite of the apple, and then the snake that wrapped itself around her, what do you see? (l+S=$) Do you see it now? I can be too prideful at times, so that was there, and when I love, I love hard and sometimes too hard. It can destroy your relationships and then your heart if you love that deeply. What are the things that you must protect above all? Your body, soul, and mind. It is amazing to love someone that much, even when they don't feel the same way, but it is our own fault, if we allow the darkness of pain to tear apart the very fabric of our core when it doesn't work out. How would I be able to let my love be shared again if I'm letting it destroy me? I'm still going to love that hard every time I find it, but I won't let it destroy me this time. Instead, I will appreciate how much strength the Lord has given to continue loving them, even when they are no longer around. After all, isn't that what he does when we turn our backs on him, or forget he is even there?

The many-faced God himself can come to you in many forms, but it's up to each and every one of us if we decide to learn the lesson that is being taught. We are stubborn children who want to do things our own way and in our time, aren't we? We need to ask for the "scales" to be removed so that we can see that the Almighty is in each one of us and start listening. The Almighty is teaching us, even when we don't realize that there is a lesson being taught. Stop waiting for this magical digital mark to appear. Go ask your Creator to show you the marks you were too blind to see. It may be hard for some to bear, and he will only show you what he knows you can handle. Some marks even change over time, as we do. After the Almighty shows you, ask for the marks to be washed off. These lessons were amazing, but I was at that point of exhaustion, yet still addicted. My Creator never left my side, though, and knew I needed rest. I was being hard on the Almighty and then myself for not seeing this a long time ago. This leads us into the next chapter.

Chapter 8

A Needed Rest and More Learned Lessons

On the last day I was at my mom's, I was told to leave. I couldn't tell them what was troubling me, and at the same time, I knew it was God's will to make me leave, no matter how it was done. If I had stayed, my journey would not have continued. I was also hurting my loved ones because they couldn't understand what I was going through, whether it was the demons I was facing and releasing or the drug that was beginning to take over my life again. The police came and picked me up one afternoon, taking me to the hospital once again. I was then committed to my next rehabilitation center, but I wasn't angry. I knew I needed the rest. My body was so exhausted, and I was so tired of fighting.

The first few nights at the hospital and then at the Old Barnyard were almost a relief, and I was grateful. My mind and body were getting rest from all the things that hurt beyond their very walls. I got to meet some other people there who were also going through some spiritual awakenings. Not everyone is at a rehabilitation center for drugs or alcohol abuse. Regardless, they had some extraordinary minds, and I liked being around them. It was almost as if there were some hidden knowledge within us all, and it was those things that made each of us special. It was our own hidden language of love meant just for people like us that we, so desperately, wanted to share with the rest of the world.

I did not stay for very long, and they gave me a ride back to my camper. There was still so much anger that had not been resolved within myself and the ones whom I hurt. It was almost a dreadful feeling to come back. The heat was so bad, and I had no electricity or running water in my camper. Not to mention, I still had the drugs that I left behind. I felt very alone, and it was too easy to relapse again. I knew the drugs were waiting for me, but I did not tell anyone. I knew it was another escape, if I needed it.

Roy was still angry at me for hurting my mom, destroying my own life, and hurting him as well. He had every right to be, and I was just too stubborn to tell them what was really hurting and hidden behind the drugs. Honestly, I didn't know how to tell them. Loneliness can destroy a person, especially those who thrive around other people. I had forgotten that I was never really alone. I was angry, and the heat was so heavy. My truck, with its keys still missing from my adventures in the woods, made me decide to just walk. I met a very nice couple who gave me a ride on the first night. I was especially grateful to them, because Nine Mile Road at night is dark and dangerous for anyone to be walking.

    I walked from my mother's and back to my friend's house and then many other places after. My friend wasn't there, so I was stranded in the middle of Havelock, in the middle of the night. I walked from Walmart, which was closed, down to the hotel closest by. I rested there when a stranger came out and gave me some water. He has no idea how much that water helped. I didn't have the money to stay at the hotel, so I began to walk again. Not knowing where I was going, another stranger pulled up beside me. He rolled down his window and asked if I needed anything and if I was OK. I looked at him, and for a second, I hesitated. Then I realized he was exactly what God had sent into life in my time of need. He was a black man, and I thought to myself, I am not a scared white woman of my very own brother, and I quickly said, "No, I am not OK." I got in his truck, and the first thing I noticed was the angel sitting on his dash, and I knew right away that I was safe.

    Can you imagine that lesson? The black man saves the white woman without asking for anything in return, and I hesitated. I knew what lesson I was being reminded of. I never hesitate when it comes to race or the differences in our skin color, and I wasn't going to start that night. I knew without a doubt that there are angels all around us, in every shade; we just have to let ourselves see it and stop being so afraid. He helped me over the next couple of days and even helped me hot-wire my own truck. No, this was a Christian man, and he did not know how to do it. I looked it up myself on YouTube.

So then began my next lesson. The last night I was at my camper, I decided I was going to check on my friend. She is my sister from another mother, and I looked at that mother as my second mother, many years ago. I thought to myself, "I need to make sure she was OK." I drove to Greenville and down the very road I knew she lived on three times, but that night I could not figure out which house that was. I couldn't understand at that point, but I know now, I wasn't meant to find her that night. I wasn't strong enough. So I drove to her mother's house and knocked, but no one was home. I thought a lot about my "second mom" and how I had hurt her in the past. I wanted her to be there, so I could tell her how sorry I was, for ever leaving and hurting her the way I did. She taught me how to be a mother, too, just as my own mother did. I wanted her to know that and how much I really appreciated everything she did for me. I also wanted to tell her that she helped raise my babies, and at the very least, I could try to help her save hers.

I knew at that point that once I got well enough and strong enough to say no, I was going to be there for them, to help them however I could, and to show them just a little bit of light. I cannot expect to save them, but even the smallest amount of light and love from a sister could be enough to show them the way when they were ready. Especially if they knew I'd be right there to help them at rock bottom.

I slept in her driveway that night, and even though she wasn't there, she made me feel safe once again. I love her so much and still think of her as a second mom to this day. The next morning, I drove into town, not knowing if I would go back home or try to reach them later. I parked at a McDonald's and began writing in my journal. It was helping me pass the time, and I didn't have any money anyway. So I just sat in the truck and wrote. Shortly afterward, this guy with frizzy, Afrolike bright-red hair with a snow-white complexion walks out. He smiled with the most beautiful smile, even missing some teeth. I loved his smile; I even fell in love with a man, not just a year earlier, who had missing teeth when I first saw him. He had a beautiful smile too.

This young fellow asked me for a cigarette and started up a conversation with me, just as if he had known me for years. He was another angel within and a guide to my next stop. We briefly told each other no hidden truths, and I discovered that he was homeless, but so very happy he was. He invited me to go eat just a little way down at the Salvation Army in Greenville. It was within walking distance, but I decided to go and drove my truck over and parked. He then walked up and said, "Well, you are here for breakfast, and if you are here tomorrow, then you should come to church." That was an amazing breakfast, and I didn't expect to stay until the next day, but again, when the Almighty wants to show you something, he will make sure that you are present.

They had a shower there that I could have used, but a nice man walked up to me, as I was sitting and eating and asked if I wanted to rest and shower at his home. I was going to take them up on their offer for a shower at the Salvation Army, but then he offered. I didn't hesitate, and some may think I am crazy, but I trusted the Almighty was there with me. I went and took a shower. He looked like he had just moved into the extremely nice apartment, and there was no furniture except in the bedroom. He said he had been there since February, but I wasn't buying it. Regardless, he made a few comments that probably would have left anyone worried. I wasn't worried, though. Maybe I was there not because God knew I needed his help, but maybe he knew the young man needed mine. I knew I needed to show some things to him that I had written in my journal that morning. I wanted him to know that whatever sins he had committed before, he didn't have to do those same sins anymore, and that he was forgiven. I also wanted him to read and understand that even he, too, could forgive whoever first hurt him.

He didn't say much after reading my journal entry and just stared, as we sat there resting on his living room floor. I didn't want to tempt him anymore, so I stood up, looked him dead in his face and said, "I am not her, but you will be a friend of mine for a very long time." A little discouraged he was, but he followed my lead, and we both got ready to leave. As we were walking to his vehicle, I heard a neighbor from another apartment yell out, "Don't get in the car with him!" I knew, though, that at that point I was protected, and I was not afraid of him. She had obviously known something about his past, but I knew that I was meant to be there.

We got in the car and left. He gave me a few tips on how to get some extra cash if I needed it by taking me to the plasma donation service. I did not give plasma that day, but it was nonetheless great advice for someone who was struggling. He took me back to the Salvation Army, and I went to get into my truck. He never once laid a finger on me. He was a black man, too, and I believe without a doubt that we helped each other that day. Although I was back at my truck, I couldn't leave because mysteriously my truck began to smoke. Still to this day, I don't know what or if anything was truly wrong with the engine, but I spent the night in the Salvation Army parking lot.

I felt safe that night, and when morning came, that beautiful man with red hair and his beautiful girlfriend approached. They invited me into church, so I went into church for the first time in many years that day. I didn't understand why the Almighty was keeping me there at that point. I even spoke to one of the ladies, a service member there. It was the first time that I had admitted to my visions and to seeing the patterns that God was showing me. It was as if she already knew, though. It was even talked about in the service that morning. I wasn't sure what God wanted me to do, and that troubled me. She couldn't give me that answer, but I felt assured either way that I would find out, in due time.

That day, I got a ride to the shelter. They had one or two beds available. No one was inside at that point, so I took a shower and began to rest. A young lady who was so sweet came in, and we talked for a short time. What bothered me was that she told me that she wouldn't qualify for an apartment because she doesn't have any mental or health issues, and funding was always provided to them before anything else. It didn't anger me that the others were provided for first, but it did anger me that we have so much money taken in taxes, and floating around in government bills and projects. Why the hell couldn't we help all of them? It didn't make any sense to me. We waste money on so many things that we know in society and government could all do without, yet we can't provide help to all those that need it. Especially the ones who were making a conscious effort to help themselves.

I looked around the room at all the bunks that were surrounded by the few belongings that they could have with them there. How selfish have we all become? I had extra rooms in my home that I didn't even use before I sold it. There are homes and mansions in this world that have rooms, sometimes by the dozens, and much more than what is really needed. How many rooms do you have in your homes that you don't even use? I felt shameful, yet here I was, taking a bed of the few that were left, and even though I couldn't get back to my camper that had no power, I still had more than what they did. I couldn't take a bed that night, especially knowing there could be someone else who needed it more. That's when I decided to get up and begin walking again. I walked all around Greenville from my truck to different places, and back to my truck again. My anger began to grow again, as I thought about all these people who have nothing to give but still give whatever they have if you need help.

I took off my shoes once again and walked until I could take no more of the hot pavement. It was as if I were doing the penance of my sins for not seeing this sooner. I did get a pair of tennis shoes one afternoon, but they were too big, and I figured someone may need them more, so I left them on the top of a trash can, right where I knew some of the homeless would walk past. I walked the streets for the next few days, meeting yet two more angels sent to protect me during the night. Can you guess what I will say next? They both were black men with no hidden agendas and who didn't see color but saw a sister in need. I am grateful for all of them who were there to help me and teach me, even if I didn't realize it at the time.

Regardless of what I was learning, I was still an addict and was using that crutch to mask my pain. The only thing running through my head at that time was the fact that I knew at this point how scared I had been on the streets, yet someone made sure to guard me as I slept well, under the roof they provided. I know in my heart I would do the same. I would give up my bed and stand guard at the door all night if it meant that they could sleep feeling safe for just one night, if I had the chance. Can any of you say that you would do the same? I believe that all of you could find that kind of compassion in your hearts. Would you give up your bed or extra room if it meant allowing the comfort of safety for just one night to someone who needed it, without any judgment toward them? One night can give just a little glimmer of hope to anyone. Challenge yourselves to go to the very shelters where they stay and spend the night. Get to know them, and if you are willing, guard them while they sleep.

I was hurting for them at this point. The pain from the year and a half prior and the pain of learning who I truly was, as I was being

MY FALL FROM GRACE

taught by the Almighty himself, was too much. Sometimes it takes looking at yourself and seeing what is ugly on the inside, so that way, you can tear it down and build it back up with something new from the inside out. It only took those last few days in the heat, with all the pain I was encountering and being strung out from drugs, for me to call the ambulance on myself. Stupid me. Or was it subconsciously a way to stop the cycle? I forgot that I had my drugs on me. They knew I had them, but I am a feisty one, and they didn't find them the first few days in the hospital, but I knew it was coming. I had already accepted my fate when I arrived at the rehabilitation center the first night.

Obviously, they search for your belongings to make an account of everything you bring in. I didn't lie to the officer, either, who was called, and I was honest from the start. This was my first real trouble landing me with a charge. I didn't even have a driving record at that point. They didn't take me that night because I needed the detox and mental health help from the facility, but they came within a few days. I was charged with felony possession of meth. I was scared, but at the time, I was willing to take whatever punishment they deemed fair. The first two nights, my anxiety was high, and all I wanted to do was get out. My bond was only $1,500, so I could have bailed out with $250. I am so grateful to my brother and mom who stood their ground and said no.

I finally calmed down, and after a few days, my cellmates grew to like me just a little. They were hard on me, but I was different, and maybe they saw the privileged color of my skin and resented me a little. That's why I didn't get angry with them. I liked them all a lot, whether they realized it or not. During my two weeks, I began to read. I read five books in just a two-week period, fitting a few card games in between. I know you guys cheated at first, but you were teaching me the game and how to really pay attention. Thank you, guys, for that. I was meant to be there, to read those books. One was a very special one, by a very well-known author in the urban world. He spoke to me through his book, and it was as if I was exactly where I needed to be to find it. So thank you, Tony Evans, for writing the book, *My Comeback*. You inspired me again, and you reminded me that I had come back from worse situations, and I could do it again. You were another angel on my journey, whether you knew it or not. They all were!

I went to court for my second appearance and got time served, since I had never been in trouble before. I left that afternoon and had no idea how I would get home. About two hours after getting out, my cellmate walked out. She was such a sweet girl, a little deviant, but aren't we all? I stayed for my first time in the trap house that night. No, I am not telling you where that is. Some things you just must leave unspoken. In any case, I learned from being there how to survive without water. You see, they had enough money to pay for electricity but not the water bill. I completely understood choosing electricity over water. It kept them cool when the heat was too much to bear.

I also got to see all the addicts who were from different backgrounds, but they were no different from me. One person brought me breakfast the next morning. He walked to go get it, if that tells you anything. One very handsome fellow offered to take me home that day. I have a few promises that I intend to keep once I am back working because he not only showed compassion for a sister in need, but he was also extremely patient with me. They all were. This is where another chapter begins, but I will never forget the lessons that I learned in my times of darkness and what faces showed up to help. You were all angels in your own ways, and I know you were there because the Almighty knew that I needed you.

Chapter 9

Thor's Hammer and Forgiveness

When I first arrived back in Havelock, I stopped by my brother's house, who initially said I could stay there. I didn't respond when he said angrily, "Why are you here?" Instead, I walked out angry and hurt at the same time, never saying a word. I went to my camper, and I slept there with no electricity or running water. At first, I felt lost but grateful that I still had a roof over my head. Those next couple of days were hard, and I didn't get high right away, but the heat and anger grew, and I caved. I looked for the pipe that I knew had some drugs left in it. I knew there were a few of them. I couldn't remember where all of them were, but I found one. I got high that night, and then I felt like a failure.

MY FALL FROM GRACE

My cousin was just there a few days before, and he knew my struggle. He had even bought me $80 worth of food and water. I was angry at myself at this point, so I did exactly what I needed to do. I went outside the camper. I got the hammer of Thor itself (it was Stanley hammer), and I took the wet rag that I used with water to cool myself and that my cousin blessed me with to wrap up that pipe. I then took that hammer and did the hardest thing I have had to do yet, and I busted that fucking pipe into a million pieces, with every piece locked inside the wet towel. That hand towel never had a chance and is buried within the trash that I will never speak of again. If I can gather the strength for that kind of power, then so can any of you. Use that hammer when you are ready, and destroy the son of a bitch! I have faith in you all!

Afterward, that is when things started to get better, and they can for you too. I wasn't mad at my brother or anyone else who closed their door to me. I knew at this point that this was exactly the way it was supposed to be. I had to do this part alone, and no one else could make me do it. I had many people helping me, though, whether I knew it or not, or they knew it or not.

I began to see even more of the beauty of our Lord in everything. He spoke to me through the songs that I was listening to, and I could see all his many faces in everything. I was finally listening to sounds all around me. My eyes were opened, and the "scales" were falling off, little by little. All I wanted at that point was forgiveness, not just from the Almighty but also from myself and others whom I had hurt. Not just the ones that I had hurt recently but also throughout my whole life. I guess this is me saying I am sorry in my own way, to all those people. All the way back to grade school.

I wasn't just the victim of a bully; I became the bully at times. I am so sorry for anyone whom I may have hurt. I am so sorry that I never went back to make amends to the girl who thought I threw rocks at her car. I promise you with all my heart that I never did that to you. However, I did take part in doing it to someone else whom I once loved. I was guilty, regardless, and I was guilty of envying you, whether you knew it or not. I still, from time to time, look at how beautiful you really are, and I hope that one day we can become friends, because that's really all I ever wanted.

I thought about my children and how I have hurt them. I never meant to, and I am so sorry for not standing strong, but I will tell you this: my weakness and failures have given me a new strength, and I know you will still be proud of your mom. I thought about my sisters (all of them) and my brothers (all of them too). You see, we might not be from the same bloodline, but we are if you take it back to the beginning and turn water into wine, right in our very own veins. I thought about my parents, my friends, my old neighbors, and my family in the work world. I knew they all knew something was wrong. Who was I fooling? You can't hide that! Especially from the people who love you the most. I am so sorry to any of you that I hurt or let down. I promise you all, when you see me next time—and I hope that is very soon—that you see someone who is recovering. I also hope for your forgiveness.

MY FALL FROM GRACE

What I am grateful for are all of you and the knowledge to know how good each one of you really are. I am grateful for the hard lessons, and the people in health care who help people like me, even when we are out of our minds. I am grateful for the police officers and EMTs; I am grateful for my time in jail and the judge who reduced my charge and gave me time served. No offense, but if I see you again, it won't be in a courtroom. I am grateful to my family and their forgiveness for what I put them all through. My mom and Roy even provide me shelter now, as I still go through this healing journey.

It's been one hell of a journey, and I'm just getting started, but we are just about done with this book. The next chapter brings me to talk about the real pain that still hurts me today. It is the chapter that is the designated end and is followed with my new beginning. Maybe a new beginning for all of us…

Chapter 10
My Person

The man I fell in love with, most of my family and friends hate today. I still to this day love that man with all my heart. He was my best friend, and I miss him greatly. Now you all can blame him for my addiction, but he didn't make me do it, and I was clean when I got home. It was my choice and my choice alone, whether tempted or not. Yes, those drugs can make you crazy and out of your mind. I saw that in myself, so I'm sure you all remember. Even when we did things that hurt each other, I knew it wasn't the man or who I really was because we got to know each other sober too. You never saw that side of him. You never got to see the pain behind his very eyes.

You see, he lost his twin flame. He loved her so much, and she died. Just so you know, he did not kill her, and that was verified to me by the officers directly on the case. That pain, no matter how it's lost… it never leaves. I know because I can feel that very pain in my soul. He used that drug to mask his pain, not knowing or realizing who he was hurting. He had known so much pain throughout his entire life that he didn't know how to accept a love like mine. Can you imagine a life without love like that? How will you be able to forgive me for doing the exact same things, if you can't even forgive him?

I began to realize what I had questioned our Creator about just weeks before, when I asked why he hadn't forgiven the fallen son. That's how I know that, without a doubt, he has! The love never leaves when you love someone that much, no matter what they did to hurt you or what you did to them. It never leaves! Do you know that even when we turn our backs on God, forget he is there, or blame him, he never stops loving us? The answer is: he will never stop! He continues loving us, no matter how badly we hurt him every single day.

I then began realizing just how bad our Creator must be hurting inside. Yes, he knows joy from the ones who love him, but he still hurts for the ones who are lost. What parent wouldn't? So, with that said, I still love him regardless, just as I love all of you, and it doesn't matter if I wasn't the one person for him. I want him to be happy, and I can love him from afar with the ability to love the way I do, with the love I was gifted with from the Almighty. I also believe that thee love sent from up above down into my very heart will be enough to send the energy directly to his, and maybe he, too, can begin to heal from the inside out.

I pray for him like I would anyone else, every single day. I pray for the Almighty himself too. I pray that one day all of us can unite as one and go home together so that we, too, can stop his hurting. I ask you to find it in your hearts to do the same. We are no different, and no sin is greater than the other, so if you are going to forgive, I am begging you to forgive him too. Whether you knew who he really was behind all the pain and drugs that he hid behind, I got to see the goodness in him too. We all deserve a second chance, don't we?

The pain of losing someone is getting easier to bear, but knowing that I can still love and forgive him and myself for the wrongs that we did to each other gives me peace. I don't ever want to be that person who is afraid to love like that again. He will always be a part of my history, and I am grateful for that. What you also didn't see is that he was there for me every single day during my cancer and recovery. He kept me grounded when I needed to refocus, and he showed me how to be myself again because I had forgotten who she was. I was so wrapped up in working every single day, wearing the same things, indulging in the profits, but never having time for myself, for my children, my friends and family, and to show off that free spirit I always used to be. He allowed me to see that in myself again.

And understand this: if it weren't for him, I never would have learned these lessons and come back to Christ. I always knew and loved Christ but never really had a relationship with him until now. I talk to him every day, not just in prayer, but like he is kickin' it right there with me, as we drive with the radio up on full blast. You see, even the ones that we cast out and call demons can really be a guide back into light when we have lost our way. Maybe there were never any demons at all. Maybe that is what I chose to see. Maybe they, too, were there to help me, even when I thought they were demons that surrounded my home before I sold it. You weren't demons at all, and I know without a doubt, you were there to get me out of that house, so I could begin my journey. I am grateful to all of you. You helped save my life. I am sorry I didn't see that sooner.

Now that I have gotten that out of the way, I still see the numbers and patterns in everything. You obviously know by now that I am a researcher, an investigator, and a slight stalker, so I now have the addiction where I want to know more. I researched different religions, different meanings behind the numbers, humankind, and the history of life and its meaning, and knowing who I truly am. I have been researching things for the last six years, and even in my failures, I never stopped wanting to know more. I just simply got a little off subject for a while. This is what is going to bring you to my last and final chapter. Remember what I said before: my last chapter in this book is my beginning. Are you ready now to see my beginning? I knew you would wait!

Chapter 1:1

My Beginning and My Twin Flame

We are not going back to the very beginning because you know my history by now. I have always been a warrior and fought through many battles. I became homeless after leaving my husband to have a beautiful home on the river in only eleven years and did this as a single mom. Now I didn't do that on my own entirely. I must give credit where credit is due. My family helped so much. I had great mentors and fellow teammates who became family and taught me to push myself and friends who also were family and always had my back. And I had the Lord, even when I forgot about him at times. I am honored to have those people in my life because without them, I may not have succeeded. It did take a lot of strength and willingness to prove to myself and the ones who may not have believed in me that they were wrong. I am very proud of myself for that. That's where it begins for me. If I can do that, I can achieve anything, and so can you!

We all have a warrior within us; you just must find where they are resting. That's where I found who my twin flame really is. Let me explain. Through all this, I realized the patterns and the numbers and what they were telling me. You see we look up to the Trinity: the Father, the Son, and the Holy Ghost (or whichever names your culture uses). And what do you think that the Triangle or the Trinity as one unit looks down and sees? Take a moment if you need it. It looks like a reflection of itself. What do you get with the perfect triangle, and the reflection of another perfect triangle on the other side? By now you should realize, you see a square. All perfectly balanced and within the square, two perfect triangles. We are the reflection of our Creator. The all-seeing eye above looks down and sees the all-seeing eye below, looking back at it.

What else do you think is seen in the reflection? We *all*—human, animal, plant, insect, fish, waters, the earth itself, and all the material within it—are the creations of the Almighty. That includes the very cars that you drive. The Creator is everything because all things that we are and use are the very materials and DNA that the Almighty created. Now here comes the tricky question: What do you see when you look up at the reflection looking down at you? Ask now to remove "scales." Whether it happens right away or over time as the Creator knows you may need, the Almighty will show you, if you ask.

This is what I know. I see my own reflection and the Creator on the other side. I look up or down, from side to side, and directly into the mirror itself. I see the Creator above and everything that was created as the greatest Architect of all time looks down and sees. You want to know what else I see? I will tell you this. I see the lion that roars over the pride land. I see the elephant with ears big enough to hear from every corner of the galaxies. I see the lamb that is so gentle, it gives us all comfort. I see the cat that gets too curious at times but still loves unconditionally. I see the dog that has become the best friend, and who doesn't love a good "dog park"? Laugh because it's funny. I see the giraffe that stands tall to eat from the tops of trees, while leaving the fruit at the bottom for us shorter ducklings to eat. Hey, Duckie, I miss you!

I see the tall deer with its antlers standing up even higher and showing its age with a dozen of its points. I see the spider that only comes out at night to weave its beautiful web, only to retreat by morning. I named my pet spider Hector. I see even an irritating gnat that sometimes just wants a sip from the eyes, or maybe they are there to help remove the scales itself. I see all the beautiful animals that were created, including the snake because it is beautiful too. I see the fly that lands upon us and only wants us to see; it's just as beautiful as the butterflies are. I see the Joker setting off a bomb in the office and the grizzly bear (the big teddy bear he is) saying, "You're such an ass!" I see both man and woman, both brother and sister and child. I see all my sisters on the other side of the United States and both of my brothers here and on the other side of the world. I see sisters that are blooded by choice and all their beautiful hair choices. I see my mothers and fathers. I see all of you and, and I see myself. I see all my ancestors back to the very original bloodline of my own, in Ghana, Africa, and boy, are they beautiful too!

I see my children because they are "my little grasshoppers"! Boys, I hate to tell you, but when you bring them into my life, they are my daughters, too, and I see all of them as well! I miss them just as bad! We *all* are the reflection that our Creator sees, and we must know that when we look at a reflection, or down or in front of our faces, for that matter, we have to see exactly what is seen on the other side. We are the Creator, and the Creator is in us *all*. From the very beginning of time. If we look up or directly into the mirror itself and see only one part of our reflection, we are ghosts or nothing at all. Don't you get it? *We all* and the Creator are one. That is what makes the square.

What is needed to make a steady, stable, and safe church for all to dwell within? You must have all four sides. We are the fourth side to the church that is waiting to be finished. Can you look at your neighbor, friend, or foe and see yourself in them? Can you look at all the beautiful animals, plants, and minerals and see yourself in them? That's how we build the church. That's the New World Order we should all be looking for. Both good and bad people can be either good or bad people, all at the same time. It's in all of us, including our reflections. We have to love, even the darkest parts of ourselves. Because if you don't, your heart will never be a complete heart, and there will always be pain.

I discovered who my twin flame truly is. It's me, myself, and I. It's my reflection, it's all of you reading this now, it's the loved ones and animals that we've lost since the beginning of time until now, and it's everything else all around us. You must really see within, from the top of the house to the bottom, from each side left and right, up and down. That is the all-seeing eye. The eye that sees everything on the outside and yet sees everything within oneself too. It's within you and your very heart and soul as well. That's where you are going to find the Creator.

I know and believe in all of us, from the politicians and world leaders who bicker and fight like kids every day, to the ones who are still suffering and have lost their way. We all have the power to look in the reflection that is staring back at us. Once we all discover that it's all of us—not one man left behind to decide to unite as one and build the church together—only then will the bride and bridegroom be united. I didn't have to go all the way to Israel to tell my dream. Israel is within us all.

Now do you understand? This is the beginning of a new beginning for us all. I am not Christ; I am not a Savior or a prophet. I am a Sinner, and I am no different from you. I am you, and all of you are me from the top of the house to the bottom of the house. We teach it until we finally get it right. There is a patriot in all of us. What kind of patriot will you be? A patriot who only fights for one half of the house or will say, "Never again" and fight for all of humanity? *I am a patriot for us all, and I don't own any weapons! My weapon is my heart filled with love! My sword is my pen, and my voice is my Creator and my own reflection!* Who is ready to lay down the weapons of anger and pick the weapons up called "tools" (I owe somebody some tools, by the way), to help build the church back up to its rightful standing? I am still healing, but the one thing that I have always found in life is that it is so much greater when you are helping others and healing together.

Will you be patriots for all? I know you all will stand united as one with me! I have that kind of faith! We have a lot of work to do, so I need your help. *I know who I am. Do you know who you are now?* There is a Creator in all of us. We all have that power. We are the nation of nations! Can we call that unity?

Thanks to all of you. And are you ready to start a new beginning, even after an ending? I love you all from the bottom of my heart, from this side of the world, all the way to the other! Let's break the chains that bind us. Let's turn Aarons cane back into the beautiful snake he was, so he can become the "8," bringing the "6" and "9" back together again! Do you see it now? The perfect yin and yang. (My brother is laughing right and saying in his *Beavis and Butthead* voices he used to do, "Sixty-nine! Sixty-nine! Huh, huh! She said sixty-nine!") We can all be dragon queens and kings if we want! Go out in the sunlight when it is shining, and if it gets too hot, take shade under the weeping willow or climb up and take a rest on the limbs of the great white oak itself.

If you want to dance or make love in the moonlight, do it! Take your dog out for a walk, even at night. Let him off the leash if wants to run, because they always know how to find their way back home! Just don't get lost in the shadows as the Phantom did for too long, because the sunshine will miss you way too much! It's OK to love both sides! I do! And, brother on the other side of the world, I'd love to come visit you sometime. And hell yeah, we are going to sky-dive together! Maybe I can bring my sis, if she is daring enough! Sis, it's time for a vacation! Maybe we can pick up my other sisters on the way!

This is not the end, remember. Now go outside and say, "Good morning, good day, or good night, beautiful," because no matter what part of day or night, the darkness is just as beautiful as the light. That is the balance within and the way to build the church back up.

Also, I loved working in the car business because it taught me so much, but my real dream would be to work at the United Nations itself. Let this be my résumé, and maybe it will find its way into the right hands. What I have learned about myself is that no matter what job I have worked at, over the last twelve years, is that everyone comes to me as a momma bear for advice when they need it. I had some good mommas who taught me. Maybe you can create a "Momma Bear" position for me. That way, when all of you world leaders can't sit down and talk to each other without resentment or shutting your mouths long enough to hear what the other person has to say, I can step up and teach you, just as my first mother taught me. Sit down, shut up, and hold hands. Hold hands until you can forgive each other, and no squeezing the other person's hands either! Once you have calmed down, then maybe you can ask the questions that really matter. What are your children's names? What have you been taught by your fathers? What do you like to do in your free time? What struggles have you seen in your families, homes, and cultures? What's your favorite food? Can we do a potluck next time we meet because that sounds good? Can you bring your family with you? Oh, what the hell, let's just take a break today, go outside, and play a good game of kickball! Doesn't that sound more fun anyway? I promise, it will be a fun and laughable day! Then we can all come back in and really discuss how this nation of nations can work it out! I believe it could happen! After all, I am the author of my own story! Maybe one day, I'll get to look directly into the face of the F-35 itself. I was once told how mighty it looked as it stared down at you! Hmm, maybe I already have...

Oh, and who let the dogs out? I need my pack back! We have to get started working, and I am just rambling at this point! I was never really a writer anyway! I need a scribe.

With love from,

A girl with a sunshine heart and warrior's soul, who loves to dance in the moonlight!

You can just call me "Ma," though, or Bruh, Sis, Bitch, Sunshine, Meth Addict in Recovery, the Rock Bitter, Lilly, Medusa (yes, someone in rehab called me those names), Am (short for Amber, and nickname given by brother), Amber Dawnel, Amber Stroud, Amber Doyle, Amber Dawn, Frick or Frack (I could never figure out who was whom, Beth, but who cares…I will just be your stalker because I love you), the Hamburglar, or Warrior Queen, because I am all of those! I am me, but you can call me whatever you feel is necessary that day!

After all, I do love apples! I'm still waiting to try some of those famous granny brownies with that special twist!

(Oh, and I miss my best friend, and if he will forgive me, maybe a judge somewhere will let me and all my other brothers and sisters do some time for him. Just so his sentence isn't so long. We all failed him, anyway, when we forgot that it takes a village to raise a child and let him go astray. Maybe he will find it in his heart to forgive me, and I can look into his eyes once more. Maybe the president himself will set him free, just like we all know he is going to do for his own child! Get mad if you want, but you know it's true, and you would do the same for yourself and your child! Punish him by getting creative if you want to. Maybe he can cut the grass for you at the White House until it's time for you to move out, whether this term or next. After all, isn't that what the Almighty would do, if asked for forgiveness?)

I really do love that man and I'd accept any type of relationship with him, just to have him back in my life!

Humanity Challenge!

Here is my challenge to all of humanity: go and write your own gospels of truth, because we are all sinners, but we can make a butterfly effect so big that it creates a whole new world. We can call that *The Book of Life* and create the heaven we have all been waiting for! Maybe, if anything is possible, I can send this book back in time so that it can create all the beautiful stories that remind me of who I really am! I just have to believe it, and I believe with all my heart! No, I don't have the heart of a cowardly lion either! I have the heart of a lioness that loves everyone as if they were her own! That is a mighty and strong heart! Hear me roar! That means that all of you already read this story! Can we celebrate now because I am done writing? It's a beautiful day in the neighborhood. Won't you be my neighbor! I love you all, cousins!

To all you spiritual leaders around the world, it doesn't matter what religion, but take your churches and temples out into the streets next Sunday or every day if that's what it takes! Preach your sermons in the streets, and let the chorus or bands play everywhere. Just like we long to hear the angels sing, they long to hear the angels down here sing too! If you are shut inside, then the ones who never get close may never hear you! Those are the ones who may need to hear whatever guidance and mentorship you share. You'd be surprised who would stop and listen, even if you don't see them sitting there in the darkness. Can we have church outside for a while? After all, the church is everywhere in all of us, from the top to the bottom and left to right! Sing, because that is the frequency that brings new life!

If there is anyone who will help me start a nonprofit dedicated to the kids. I want to call it Big Brother, Big Sister Mentorship. No matter how hard anyone tries as a single parent, we cannot give them what they need as mother or father if the other is missing. Not just a mentorship that ends at the end of a five o'clock day, but mentors who stick with these kids for life so that our children can get the best of both worlds. They need it, and I even saw that in my own children. Someone they can call, any time of the day or night. Whether it's to teach them how to be a man or how to braid hair, because their fathers try the best they can, but let's be honest: there is nothing like a woman's touch. Is there anyone out there who will help me start that kind of nonprofit? A village, right?

For my final request and challenge, I triple triple-dog-dare you to stand in the closest mirror and sing, "Good Morning, Beautiful" because that is exactly what you all are! And please, post those videos if you want, because if you do, I will find the strength to do the same.

Milton Keynes UK
Ingram Content Group UK Ltd.
UKHW021153240724
445899UK00014BA/646